Thoughts Painted in Black and White

By: Chrishonda "Chris Crawford" Smith

1

Author Photo by Kari Smith
Cover Design and Photos by Chrishonda Smith

ISBN 979-8-9926958-0-9
Library of Congress Control number 2025903071
Printed in the Unites States

Dedication

I would like to dedicate this collection of poetry to my family. Thank you for your support, love, and inspiration during this journey. I Love you ALL more than words can express. Each of you played a vital role in making this book a reality. This is for my family here in the flesh and those who guide my pen in spirit.

Intro

Thoughts, the process of using your mind to think of something. My thoughts reflect my experiences on this journey we call life. The good, the bad, and the in between. Please enjoy reading my thoughts along the way.

TABLE OF CONTENTS

6

TICK-TOCK CLOCK

All my thoughts are jammed packed in my head
I want to write them down, but I can't seem to
move my thoughts from head to paper
It's like my thoughts are locked
Stop ticking clock
Maybe if the clock stops ticking, I can get my
thoughts unlocked
Every time I think I've got something, the sound of
the clock gets louder, tick-tock, tick-tock
Why does the clock have to go tick-tock?
Tick-tock, tick-tock, tick-tock
Stop ticking clock, so I can unlock my thoughts
Stop ticking clock
I think I'm going to scream
Why does that clock have to be so mean
That ticking sound will not stop

Ok, I'm just going to ignore it so that I can create a
coherent thought
It's driving me insane this ticking clock
This ticking sound has me talking to a clock
Stop ticking clock, just STOP
Why is that clock ticking so loud
I'm trying my best not to just smash this ticking
clock
Calm down self, it's just a clock
Tick-tock, tick-tock goes the clock
With every tick of the clock, the longer my thoughts
are locked
With every tick of the clock, the harder it
is for those thoughts to be unlocked
I want to write down all the thoughts I feel swirling
in my head
But that ticking clock's battery just won't go dead
The tick-tock sound of the clock has me seeing red
I'm so upset that ticking clock is holding my
thoughts captive

If it wasn't for this ticking clock, I could release my
thoughts
Tick-tock, tick-tock, tick-tock
There must be something wrong with this clock.
I've never heard a clock so loudly tick-tock
I'm so tempted to crawl under my desk, so that I
don't have to hear that annoying ticking clock
To unlock my thoughts, that ticking sound
I'm going to have to block
But I can't block out that ticking clock
Tick-tock, tick-tock all around the clock
All around the clock, tick-tock
That ticking sound is burying those thoughts deep
within
When will that ticking sound come to an end
And the flowing of my thoughts from my head
down to paper can begin
I promise I won't let this ticking clock win
I'm going to slowly breathe out, then slowly breathe
in

Then count backwards starting from ten
Ten, nine, eight, seven six, five four, three, two one
Nothing
Ticking still goes around the clock
It just won't stop, this ticking clock
The ticking clock mocks
Tick-tock, tick-tock, tick-tock
So frustrated, I try again slowly breathe out, then slowly breathe in
As I count again starting from ten
Ten, nine, eight, seven, six, five for, three, two, one
Tick-tock, tick-tock, still goes the sound of the clock
But the sound of the tic-tock no longer controls my thoughts
Now the thoughts in my head can be unlocked
Because I finally beat that ticking clock

THOUGHTS

Sitting, thinking, wishing, hoping, worrying,
All these emotions running through my head at the
same time
Trying to figure out what to do, where to go, how
far to go
If I should go at all, Should I just run away from it
all
Go to a place where I can just forget about all my
worries, concerns, problems, and pain
I don't know
Time is passing by so fast, yet slow at the same time
The days seem pretty much the same
Go to work then come home
But the problems and worries they grow bigger and
stronger everyday
It seems like everyone around me is doing things so
much better and faster

Their dreams are becoming reality now, while mine are still stuck in my head

I see them, to me they seem close, yet still so far away

Why can't my dreams become reality right now

Why do I have to wait until tomorrow, and another tomorrow and another tomorrow, and yet another

When will my tomorrow be today

I think about these things every day and yes, I know I sound selfish with all this me, me, me and my problems this, my worries that, but really in some way we are all a little selfish

But don't get me wrong, I care about others, my family and friends, I want their dreams and hopes to come true,

But I feel if my dreams and aspirations come true FIRST then, I can help those around me make theirs come true too

I know that is a little selfish too.

That's what I ask God, what should I do?

I can't quite hear his answer, or maybe I just can't
understand it yet,
But I know he is talking to me I can make out some
of his words, but they get jumbled in my head and
mix with my thoughts and the thoughts of others
that are in my head
I know if concentrate hard enough and pray long
enough then I will be able to understand all of his
words and can forget about all the worries,
concerns, problems, and pain in my life and focus
only on what God has in store for me
This is my ultimate goal
So, I am still sitting, thinking, wishing, and hoping
But worrying has been replaced with praying

OVERCOMING FEAR

Sitting on the edge of a ledge so overcome with fear
Knees shaking, heart racing, palms getting sweaty
Eyes looking down towards the ground, and knees
begin to shake some more
Seeing others do it so easily, with no fear, and
wondering
Why is it so hard for me
Voices yelling you can do it, Go, Go
I don't know why, but the voices of encouragement
only create more fear in me
Maybe because I'm afraid of disappointing those
who believe in me
Ok, three, two one Go! I tell myself, but myself just
won't go
Again three, two, one, Go! I tell myself, but myself
still won't go
Again three, two, one GO! I tell myself again, yet
myself still says NO
Can't you just push me, I ask, but the answer I
receive is no
You must do it yourself, But I say myself won't go

I'm asked, what's the reasons you won't go
The reasons I won't go, I really don't know
All I can think of is undeniable fear
Fear of what they ask, my answer I don't know
Do you really want to do this?
Before I answer I ask myself, "Do I want to do
this?" My answer is a resounding YES
Yes, I want to do this, and have this experience
I don't want to look back and know I let this
experience pass me by
I don't want to look back and always ask myself
Why?
I don't want to look back and say what if…
Tell yourself to do it and just do it
So, I say Self you're going to do this
Yet, I still do nothing
You can't lie to yourself, have faith and know that
God's protection will carry you through
Know God's mercy is greater than your fear
And suddenly something sparks in me, God is
always with me, he will never leave, nor forsake me,
and if I have faith like I say I do, there is no room
for fear

I think about all that God has brought me through
All the things that God has allowed me to do
As I thought, why should I be afraid to experience
something new
So again, three two, one GO! And I finally went
As I'm going, I hear cheers
As I'm going, I feel my fear has disappeared
As I'm going, I feel free because fear no longer has
control over me
God wrapped his arms around me and released my
fear
Though first I was overcome with fear
Thanks to God, my fear I overcame

THIS BEAT

Sitting quietly in my seat
I begin to hear a strange new beat
And immediately I start to tap my feet
Really feeling this strange new sound
It's like there's no one else around
All I can hear is the sound of this beat
Bobbing my head to the rhythm of this beat
Closed eyes imagining the process of creating this
beat
Suddenly my eyes open and I look around
Why is no one else feeling this sound?
Why aren't their heads going up and down?
Why am I the only one tapping my feet?
Everyone else is sitting motionless in their seats
Am I the only one that can hear this beat?
Maybe God provided me with this very special treat
Maybe there is a reason that God has for me and
this beat to meet
Maybe it's only meant to be heard by a few chosen
elite

And if that's the case, I appreciate that because this
beat is so sweet
It's like this beat has a mind of its own
Man, this beat can really stand alone
There's truly no need for this beat to accompany
any song
To add this beat to a song would be completely
wrong
This beat that says more to me than any words
could
This beat is telling me to come this way
This beat that only I can hear
This beat that was created just for my ears
I hear this beat so clear
This beat is somehow drowning out my fears
This is no ordinary beat
This beat was created to make me tap my feet,
No, rather to make me move my feet
It was created to get me out of my seat
And realize that my life needs to move to the
rhythm of this beat
I'm so grateful that God provided me with his very
special treat

I give thanks to God for allowing me and this beat
to meet
This beat is creating in me a brand-new heartbeat
Ready for all that comes along with experiencing
this strange new beat

HAPPILY EVER AFTER

Seeking my happily ever after
In my head, I've built up this perfect life
Consisting of me creating what I thought to be the
perfect plan for me
In attempts to seek out my happily ever after
I begin to realize that I don't know what I'm
Happily, Ever, After
For so long I've allowed this fictious life to become
my reality
Immersed myself in this make-believe fantasy
Conjured up an enchanted land where everything is
flawless
Indulged in this mystical reality
Made up this character in my head
And pretended that this character that I was playing
was real
Played the role so well that the real me was
concealed
Trapped inside of this self-invented fairy tale
Afraid to come out to see what my real story tells

But even more afraid to continue allowing my
destiny to be determined by what comes from this
wishing well
Wishing well, I guess this is what I'm supposed to
do next
I want to do what I know I should do, what I was
born to do
I'm finally ready to be released from this fairy tale
So, I seek God, and ask to be set free to my actual
existence
Simultaneously I ask for his forgiveness
Forgiveness, for trying to create my own plan for
my life
And allowing this fairytale to distract his reality
And for believing in this mystical unreality
Then God shows me what my real story tells
As my made-up character he conceals
And the authentic me is revealed
I now understand why I didn't know what I was
happily ever after
God didn't include in my story a happily ever after
because if I immerse myself into his plans for my
life

My story will never end and there is no need for a
Happily Ever After

NEW LIFE

I feel you moving inside of me
Changing my physical appearance
I can't dress the way I used to dress
My old clothes don't fit me anymore, now that you
are inside of me
You're growing internally, causing my mind to
expand out to places I couldn't see or reach before
you became a part of me
Now I see beyond the present, you being inside of
me forces me to look towards the future
And put the past behind me
Being in this condition is a little uncomfortable, I'm
not in control of me anymore
You've taken over
I can't sit comfortably in seats I once sat in just fine
I can't say things that once would roll off my
tongue, because you being inside of me stops me

It's uncomfortable carrying you in me, my life is not
my own
You're stretching me out, and forming a whole new
life inside of me
Every day I feel you growing bigger and stronger
The more you grow in me, the less of me I see
It's painful feeling you grow inside of me
I'm holding you in
I'm afraid if I give birth to you, it will kill me
The birth pangs are so unbearable
But I know it would hurt more attempting to
contain this new life growing within me
So, I chose to give birth to this life that's been
moving inside of me
This life that changed my physical appearance and
expanded my mind
It gave me a new vision and made me
uncomfortable
This life that I was afraid to let out

As it turns out I was right, giving birth to this new
life did kill me
But subconsciously, I think I wanted to die, because
my life before giving birth to this new life was a lie
Just a version of my deceased self, a walking corpse
I was already dead, I just needed to bury me
Say a proper goodbye in remembrance of me
As that life ends, the new life I birthed begins
I breathe out and God breathes in

THE REAL ME

Please God, I ask you right now please help me,
Search me, show me the real me, the true me
I am not this girl, that I'm portraying myself to be,
Help me God to open my eyes and see the me that
you see
The me you made me to be
Please God help me turn away and leave behind this
false me
And lead me on a journey to discover the true me
I know deep down inside she is there
Please help me to discover her, by removing all my
fears and wiping away my tears
Remove all those things and people away from me
who are just there to interfere
Interfere with the me that you want to be out here
Please take away the doubt that I have in my mind
about discovering who I really am
Please bring me strength to tread over any obstacles
that may come in my way on the journey to getting
to know the real me

Help me God to be open to receiving everything that you are about to show me
I no longer want to be that me who is afraid of getting hurt or being uncomfortable
I long to be uncomfortable and am willing to experience pain if that is what it takes to be the me that I was created to be
God help me not to feel sorry for the me I currently see,
Because I know the person I am right now, she was created to be a greater me
Take me on this journey so that I can fulfill my destiny
Fulfill my destiny, by becoming the me that you created me to be
Excited to meet the real me, the true me
The me that God molded me to be
Ready to release this illusion of me
This illusion of me that I thought was the real me
Can't wait to get rid of that me that others made me out to be
Can't wait to get rid of that me that I pretended was me

Can't wait to get rid of that me that I used to see
Eager to meet the me God created me to be
Eager to meet the me that God sees
During this journey God give me the strength to let the old me die
And give birth to the me that I have been holding inside
Let the real me come out and take the first breath of new life
Let the real me be the one to see your guiding light
Let the real me be blinded by the future you have laid out for me because it's so bright
Let the real me soar to reach your highest heights
This real me, the true me I'm ready to see
More than ready to see, I'm ready to be
I'm ready to be the me that me I was always supposed to be
The me that God always knew I would be
The me that he created specifically for me to be
I'm journeying to be that me that God already sees
Journeying to be that me, the real, true me
Here goes, false me meet the true me

Now that the false me met the true me, the false me
I no longer see.
Introducing to the world for the first time ever, the
real me

DARK THOUGHTS

I'm trying to keep it, but I'm losing my grasp
My sanity is slipping, it's being taken over by dark
thoughts
Creeping into my psyche, playing on my emotional
instability
With every passing second, I feel like I'm losing my
mental capabilities
I'm trying to fight these dark thoughts from taking
control of my mind
by taking refuge in my faith
But slowly too that's slipping parallel to my sanity
These dark thoughts are vicious, taking no prisoners
Leaving me feeling empty
I'm trying to fight this battle but around every
corner,
Another dark thought is looming
Slithering making its way into my psyche
Inviting itself into my head, taking over any other
thoughts of reason that previously lived there
Evicting them from my brain without 30-day notice

These dark thoughts put my real thoughts put my real thoughts in solitary confinement
And keep them so confined that I can't get to them
Dark thoughts bury my senses so deep I forget that that they ever existed
I forget that I once had once had sight, taste, smell, hearing, and feeling
Because now I'm blind, tasteless, can't smell, deaf, and numb
I'm clinging on to the little bit of sanity that I have left
Trying to hold on to my slipping faith, but it seems like with each tear that falls, it's slowly washing away that faith
I wipe away my tears, but they refuse to stay away
With every dark thought that crosses my mind it brings a wave of new tears with it
Dark thoughts are lurking in the shadows and anytime I feel a glimpse of hope
They crush it, squash it, and kill it
I'm trying to keep my sanity, but my emotions are taking control under the direction of these dark thoughts

31

The dark thoughts want to see me lose my mental stability by making me emotionally unstable
It's working, my sanity is rapidly slipping
Dark thoughts are spreading through my psyche like a disease
I'm trying to keep my sanity and fight off this dark thought infection
I don't know how long I can keep fighting
These dark thoughts are strong, and they're making me weak
I'm almost to my breaking point, one more push from these dark thoughts and I just may go over the edge
I'm trying to keep my faith; I'm praying so many prayers, but it seems as if God can't hear me
All my prayers keep going unanswered
These dark thoughts are clouding my mind
I try to go somewhere where the dark thoughts can't reach me
But they slither their way into my subconscious
I run from the dark thoughts, but they sprint and catch up with me
I try to lose the dark thoughts, but they find me

I walk away from them, they follow me
These dark thoughts are relentless, refusing to give
up on taking complete control over me
They want my mind, body, and spirit
I'm trying not to accept defeat, But I feel defeated
I feel like there's nothing more I can do
Please God remove these dark thoughts from my
mind
They are making me think things that I shouldn't
and say things that I otherwise wouldn't
I need these dark thoughts to go away before I do
something I will regret
God free me from the clutches of these dark
thoughts
Remove the hold they have over mind, release my
thoughts from their custody
Resurrect my senses from the grave that these dark
thoughts buried them in
Give the order to let my real thoughts of solitary
confinement
Uninvite them from my head and bring back my
thoughts of reason that lived there previously

God simultaneously catch my parallel slipping faith
and sanity and restore it back in me
Breathe life back into my decomposing thoughts
Resuscitate my psyche, stabilize my emotions and
mental capacities
Place my mind and thoughts in recovery
And give the all clear that all of the dark thoughts
have been successfully removed
God thank you for not allowing my thoughts to be
released on their own recognizances
You watched over them, turned my weakness into
strength
Now my grasp is stronger than ever, I thank you for
ICU, intensely caring unconditionally
I see you are my life's support

DIETARY PLAN

Just started a dietary plan, and every day I
contemplate how I can satisfy my hunger
I'm seeking more than just a snack
I need more than an appetizer
I don't even think that a three-course meal at a five-
star restaurant will do
Don't think they make portions big enough for my
type of hunger, Don't think I'll ever get full
Because if I ever get full
That means that I'm sedated
That means that I'm not breathing
That means that I'm unconscious
Because I can't ever see myself being so full that I
don't want to keep growing closer to God
I can never hear myself saying I've had enough of
his love,
And I could never get enough of his forgiveness,
And there is no possible way that I would ever stop
being hungry for his truth, hungry for his vision, his
purpose and his plans
I could never be too stuffed of his mercy

Or too full of his presence in my life
And how crazy would I be if I said No God
I just can't have any more peace in my life
I just don't have enough room for it right now
I want to overeat when it comes to God,
But it really wouldn't be overeating, because I'll
never get full, I can't get full
My metabolism is too high
I have a tapeworm
I need to have meal after meal after meal
I want to digest his will, I want to savor his favor
I crave his direction, I desire his affection
I delight in his protection
I say grace over our connection
And I'm starving for his satisfaction
And just to make sure that my words line up with
my actions
I'm giving up my satisfaction like a vegetarian gives
up meat
And no longer being content, with the content I use
to habitually eat
I don't care for twitter, but my new dietary plan is
something I'll tweet

Tweet because I'm so excited that being hungry is
what I'm doing right now
And my hunger is making it possible to getting me
closer for God and I to meet
Because at the end of my dietary plan
The Goal is to be invited to kneel at God's feet

BREAK FREE

The price of Freedom is expensive
But my mental health is being held for ransom
Held hostage so long, I forgot that I didn't ask to
be taken
These shackles have become ingrained in my DNA
I don't even feel them holding me back anymore
I'm lost in captivity and don't know if I've tried to
find an escape route
I'm helping my abductors keep me away from my
family
They own me, I let them
Gave me a price, I took it
Even though I know, they did not pay me my
worth
I know better, yet I stay
Imprisoned, I know where the key is
But, I'm too afraid to go get it
Also, afraid not to
Don't want to continue living in an anxious state of
mind

I told you my mental health is being held for
ransom
I can free it
All I have to do is unlock the door and find my way
home
But fear keeps pushing me back to bondage
And I surrender to its strength
It controls me, it ties me up in knots of uncertainty
Fear has chained my soul to restlessness
Wrapped my thoughts in worry and doubt
With threats of losing everything that I've worked
for
Correction everything that I've slaved for
Everything that I gave my mental health up for
Instead of paying for my release
I take bribes disguised as promotions
And just as I recognize their ploy and about to
break free
They lure me back to confinement with the promise
of a big payoff
Camouflaged as a raise, But of course it was just a
facade

Fear tactics at its best, designed to keep me their prisoner
That way I can never be free
Free to do what God's calling me to
My purpose was buried so deep within me
I didn't recognize when it tried to resurface, so it went back down again
I see a shovel, but don't realize I can use it to excavate my purpose and be free
Trapped by anxiety, and covered in stress
I'm a mess
I told you my mental health is being held for ransom
It's heavy, these shackles are heavy
I can feel them now, I feel them holding me back
Back from me, the me that I'm supposed to be
The me that God created me to be
It's heavy, carrying this worry and doubt
It's heavy, holding this fear and anxiety
It's heavy, I have to break free
It's heavy, fighting for my mental health to be returned to me
It's heavy, I'm pushing, they're pulling

40

I win, I'm free
Today I looked in the mirror and I finally
recognized me.

TATTERED WINGS

Quivering tattered wings soar in the open sky
Unable to mask this binding fear
Muzzled by silence dreading the thought of the
ensuing abduction coming my way at an accelerated
pace
Powerless against this unyielding magnetic force
demanding the relinquishment of my control
Confined to this position of stillness, restraints
strapped tightly across my body
Afflicted with the pain of discomfort
My time is not my own anymore, it's being
monopolized by strangers
Whom now have the authority to take me wherever
the wind blows
Thoughts of knowing the route of this journey have
vanished
Informed the reign of power belongs to my
capturers who have taken me along for the ride
Coerced into following their rules and regulations
to survive

42

Issued an itinerary, but the feeling of ambiguity lies
within me on whether my endurance level is high
enough to sustain this junket with breath left in my
lungs to reach my original destination
Envisioning being fearless
Fantasizing taking back the control the forces of
power compelled me to surrender
Then I realized it was just a dream, and my tattered
wings can't fly
Survival instincts kick in, begrudgingly place my life
in my abductor's hands
At least their wings are whole
To get through this ordeal, my body is numbed and
darkness spreads
Concealing any eclipse of light that attempts to seep
through the crevices left open
My psyche destroys the formation of shadows
Muted hearing, Giving my best impression of a
modern-day Helen Keller
Lurking in the darkness my mind wonders off on a
pilgrimage illuminated by glimpses of freedom, taste
hope in the air

Sweaty palms fused with salty tears create blurred
vision, and leave an aftertaste of despair
Suspended up here, thoughts of crash landings
venture through the right side of my brain
Eyes wide shut bracing myself for the onset of pain
Sending prayers up to Heaven that this torture
comes to an end
In the distance, see a sign that reads free will
coming soon
Diminished acceleration equals intensified heart rate
Down comes the nose and the rest of the body
follows, Wings extend
Increased drag produces decreased speed
Crossing the threshold of utopia
My abductors finally release me
Eyes open to see the survival of this torment with
all breath left in my lungs, made it to my destination
of origin
Gather the scattered pieces of my sanity, insert
them back into the designated areas, and breathe a
sigh of relief
You've just taken a trip in my mind of what my
imagination imagines my first airplane ride will be

THE DAY I FOUND EVERYTHING

Excitement and anticipation engulf me
Nerves start to build slowly
Check in, it's becoming real
Tagged for safekeeping, but is it really going to be
safe?
Tossed with all the others
Security check, shoes, purse in a bucket
Bare feet step across the line when given the
command
Pass to the next step
Arriving at the gate nerves increase
Call to board heart beats rapidly
Get on, find two seats together, didn't know that
would be so hard
She wants a window seat; I don't want to sit by a
window
Finally, two seats together, one by the window, the
other in the middle
We meet Jeff, whose seat is next to mine
We tell Jeff it's my first time, Jeff says he feels lucky

Calls to family, I'm secretly wondering if this will be the last time I talk to them
I tell them, I'm on and about to take off and end each call with PRAY FOR ME!
Announcements made to turn off all devices
Heart beats 30 miles per second, Fasten your seat belts
In case of emergency drills, heart beats 40 miles per second
The joking pilot makes me laugh
I'm shaking, my palms dripping with sweat
And we're off, Heart beats 60 miles per second
Eyes wide shut; all I see is the blue seat in front of me
High above the clouds, heart beats 80 miles per second
I hope I don't break these armrests
Heartbeats 90 miles per second, hitting air pockets
I stole a glance out the window
Another air pocket, heart beats 100 miles per second
Jeff gives me his drink ticket, says first ones on me

I'm flying, like I am literally off the ground, I am
not in control of me
Conquering my greatest fear
A sense of calm falls over me
I trust that God will protect me, just like he does in
my car everyday
But the sound of the flushing toilet startles me
Air pockets make me jump a little
Now back to smooth sailing, stay like this plane
please
Make me forget I'm…I don't know how many feet
in the air, yeah, I don't want to know
Wasn't too big a fan of Chardonay, but this wine is
the best I ever had
I take a sip to help me get through the air pockets,
random; What are air pockets?
Never mind, I remind myself to sip slowly
I don't want to have to get up to go to the restroom
Look out the window and imagine touching the
clouds
They look so soft; it would be ironic if they were
hard

I always thought I would have to be completely knocked out to get on a plane
But I'm completely sober, no one had to drag me, I walked on
Feeling the descent, heart beats begin to pump faster again
I can't reach out and touch the clouds anymore
The descent seems so far away, yet close at the same time
Flying over Manhattan
All my blood rushes to my fingers, I just want to write
Slightly dizzy on the descent
The plane goes back and forth and up and down
Heart almost jumps out of my chest as we land
My plan to sleep the whole way didn't happen
As I get off the plane, I'm thankful
August 22, 2012, I was reborn
Today I found everything when I lost control

BEHIND THE LENS

Behind the lens of my camera
Captured moments released
Visually telling stories
Unedited versions of life
Innocence
Candid moments in time
Having tunnel vision
Focusing on the subject
Listening with my eyes
Seeing beauty in the mess
Limitless subjects
Making time stand still
Boundless creativity
Uncensored control
Taking photographic journeys
Documenting bliss
Left eye closed
The lens becomes my only vision
Feeling emotion through each image
Saving history

I love to hear my camera click
Behind the lens of my camera is joy

ALL IN A DAY

Free falling tears streaming
Red Sweltering Eyes seeing
Angry feeling words burning
High running emotions building
Slow hurting pain flowing
Silently speaking thoughts lingering
Rapid beating heart pumping
Nervously shaking lips twitching
Uncontrollably pounding head throbbing
Loud talking voice trembling
Clutter hearing ears listening
Actively thinking mind worrying
Frustrated looking face troubling
Anxious feeling nerves increasing
Quickly happening patience decreasing
Harm causing statements stating
Half-truths telling stories creating
Meaninglessly gossiping mouths chattering
Familiar looking faces recognizing
Unexpectedly conversing couple hearing
Harmless seeming conversations having

Friends enjoying time spending
Outside sitting lunch eating
Brightly shining sun glowing

SILENCE

If a feather falls from the sky in the city,
Can you hear it? I can
I can hear the bird whimper when he loses it
I can hear sadness in his flight over the
hustle of traffic
I can hear tears fall from eyes down
the cheek of the woman with dark glasses on
Hiding her swollen and blackened eyes from
the rest of the world, as she hangs her head
walking down the sidewalk
I can hear nerves building in that student
going down the hallway with an unusually
heavy backpack
His math and science books are being held hostage
by the gun he stole from his father's safe,
He is planning to use it to pay back his bullies
I can hear cries for help from the unborn child,
whose mother chooses to smoke crack for two
I hear him beg her to stop, kicking every time
her lips touch the pipe
He longed to be normal, but now fears that's an

impossible goal to attain
I can hear the deaf man yell to the blind man that
the street wasn't clear to cross,
before he got run down by the driver too busy
texting to stop at the red light
I can hear the cashier at the grocery store regret
slipping those twenty dollars in her pocket,
as she counts her drawer down, because she can't
wait till payday to buy diapers for her baby
I can hear disappointment from the little girl,
when she realizes that all of mommy's friends
can't be her Uncle John
I can hear his hurt feelings turn into anger
When a mother tells a father that there's a reason
that their eight-year-old son
doesn't have any of his facial features
I can hear temptation leading that married man
to the doorsteps of the hotel where his coworker
turned mistress lays,
While on the other side of town,
A wife and children are waiting for daddy to
come home for dinner
I can hear the secret desires of the masses

I can hear the sound of love and distinguish it from
the sound of hate
If you listen carefully, I can be the answer to all
your concerns
I am Silence

ROOM 301

The early stench of death in the air plays tricks on
your senses
Decaying dreams and rotten eggs that never
hatched
Smell one in the same
Unattended to success becomes molded,
And now wreaks of mildew
Creating foul odors
Mr. Clean and Glade plus soiled linens equal nausea
Halitosis and body odor seeping through the cracks
underneath the doors permeates hallways
Mothballs and Lysol are used to conceal the scent
of death's cologne
But upon entrance you are doused in its aroma
There is no escaping the acidity that finds its way to
your taste buds,
When you part your lips to ask which way is room
301
Chewing on regrets leaves a bitter aftertaste of
remorse on your tongue
Swallowing liability, you choke on iniquity

And find yourself coughing up repentance
Frigid temperatures follow you to room 301
Numbing your body, Lucky you
You can't feel life escaping you slower
than the drip that drops from the IV stuck in your vein
You can't feel each memory you hold slipping out of your grasp or feel the broken smile
You wish you could put back together, just to crack
Screams behind walls excites your guilty conscience
With images of battlefields in every room,
One side has weapons needles, pills, and pillows
While the other side is left alone and defenseless
The screams are pushing through to get attention
You see outlines of faces imprinting the walls
mouthing HELP… as you walk down the hall
Fear increases your pace to find room 301
Coming to a fork in the hallway
A sign reads rooms 285-301 to the right rooms 301-315 to the left
Taking that left turn and approaching room 301 brings back your sense of feeling,
The screams behind the walls have silenced

Opening the door makes a squeaking noise,
A familiar face looks up to you and speaks
You finally made your way to see your mother
Immediately you apologize profusely
And ask, What is that awful smell in this place?
She says that's the smell of pain

THE LAST ONE STANDING

Empty nests fill the hallowed ground
Fragments of my tortured family stains my withered
branches
The pungent scent of dead oak causes weeping that
trigger leaves to fall from what remains of my limbs
Scattered twigs cover the surface
Darkness left its mark in the air
Sun has forgotten how to shine
With its amnesiac state my nutrients are non-
existent
Disintegrated trunks surround my shriveling
anatomy
Scantily, I stand alone with memories of blowing in
the wind with friends
Birds' homes nestled in my crown
Leaves changing colors with the season
Full and thick, the envy of all the land
Sunlight stretching so wide and bright none of my
fellow companions went hungry
Life growing beneath me
Severed roots, yet somehow, I remain standing
I too was planted in the ground

What was the difference in my outer bark's
protection
How was my inner bark able to produce strength in
my time of weakness
All our piths, our centers are resistant, yet they fell,
and I stand
My brethren's damage traumatized them to death
And their death is traumatizing the life out of me
Desolate, I stand in this vast territory with only my
shadow to keep me company,
And even it plays hide and seek
How did I survive the massacre that destroyed the
rest
Callous and calculating motives produced the wrath
of destruction that bulldozed my home,
And annihilated my family
Eradicated any semblance of my previous existence
with a solitary push of a button
I wonder if they realize that they just decreased time
from their own existence
Blissfully ignorant of the fact that we are the
producers of oxygen

Without us filtering the air, humans would become
extinct
I'm sure these thoughts weren't formed when the
decision was made to demolish my roots
Soil is buried under layers of concrete to ensure my
growth is forever stunted
Alone, I stand, propped up against the bricks
stacked in the center of my former home with
severed roots beneath me
There was no miracle, nothing more special about
me than the rest
I have no superpowers
I didn't survive
I just hadn't been laid to rest

UNDISCIPLINED VAGRANT

An undisciplined vagrant has more gumption
Your approach has failed repeatedly
But for some reason it's being used continually
This is the definition of insanity,
doing the same thing and expecting a different
result
How many times does one have to hit the concrete,
before coming to the realization that cement leaves
permanent scars
School must not have been something you excelled
in
Grading on the curve got you through your
formative years
Unfortunately, that's been carried into adulthood
Expecting to make it by riding the coat tails of
others
You never learned to crawl,
You specialized in running
Anything that didn't fit into your plans was tossed
aside,
like heavy trash laid out for pick up

Awaiting someone, anyone to pick up the slack you
left behind
Picking up and moving away from your
responsibilities became the theme to your existence
Bad habits contributed to your selfish nature
Actions spoke volumes to your character
Attempts were made to piece together your broken
promises
Stealing innocence and joy was your specialty
Although you were not opposed to taking hope too
Incarcerations gave you an excuse to continue
performing your disappearing act
Reappearances would occur occasionally,
Whenever the mood would strike you
Blown opportunities to make up for pass mistakes
became a part of your cycle
The nerve you had to get upset if there was no time
for you
Hurt feelings you felt, when the title you thought
you had was removed
But you never earned the right to be called Daddy,
so it was replaced with something more fitting

Sperm donor, I was only the seed you planted in my
mother
You never helped me grow
You are the definition of pusillanimous, lacking the
courage to be a father
A coward, who chose to run away from his
daughter
An undisciplined vagrant has more gumption

EVE

She uses broken logic to give into temptation
If God didn't want us to eat the apple, he wouldn't
have put it there
In plain sight, Inviting
Who amongst us wouldn't accept an open invitation
Ladies and Gentlemen, she is charged with being
polite
An unwitting accomplice allured by a sly slithering
serpent
Truth be told, she was a victim in his cleverly
orchestrated plot
I will prove that under similar circumstances any
one of you would make an equivalent decision
Rid yourselves of the fable you've been told, place
your judgement out of sight
Imagine being seduced by appearances, perfect
shape skin draped by a flawless shade of sinful red
as it hangs free
Enticed with promises of knowledge and
satisfaction once you succumb to desire

Remember, she is merely a curious young woman
being offered the ability to be God like
Isn't that what we all strive for
Testimony will show the woman was lured in by
soft whisperings of sweet nothings from a master in
disguise
Saying, you were handmade by God as am I,
You are a gift to this world as am I,
God wouldn't create something that's bad for you
If you weren't meant to have me, you couldn't see
me
I wouldn't be out in the open, taunting, enticing you
to lust for my succulent taste
I'm here to fulfill the craving that aches in you
I know you long to see everything and I want to
show you
Just reach out and grab me, I was placed here for
your pleasure pick me
Ladies and gentlemen, like many of us when
tempted this is where wrong transformed into right
in her mind
Evil tasted good

At that moment she was covered in disobedience
but unaware of its touch since she never felt it
before
Contaminated purity spread activating
decomposition of morality, infecting her and
unknowingly she transmits to him
Because of this, she's accused of spawning the
evolution of sin
Her prosecutors would have you believe that this
was a solo performance
But the truth is the serpent was the director and
man was her co-star
"I object, I played no part in this deceitful act
And anyway, God gave me this woman who forced
me to eat the apple"
Members of the jury, please note that this out of
order man has the audacity to place blame on God
Woman speaks, I am innocent, a harmless creature
created by God
Even though I came from his ribs, I still left him
scarless
It is because of me that there are members of this
jury

I gave birth to this nation inflicted with pain
because of these false accusations
Ladies and Gentlemen, the evidence speaks for
itself
There must be something special about a woman
who leaves a man perfect

MY SUPERMAN

The day I found out my hero was human
My Superman, my heart, my grandfather, he's
beaten
His kryptonite, stage 4 prostate cancer
Metastasized beyond treatment
He can't fight anymore
Yet, this is the same man I watched drop kick a
heart attack and come back stronger
His resounding will to live has
evolved into a quiet yearning for death
Kryptonite crumbled my grandfather into
fragments of himself
Some pieces move around in a disoriented state
Other parts of him use scrambled words to mutter
jumbled phrases
Home want I go to, am where I, hand grab my the
This is sad, my grandfather's words once carried so
much weight people would line up just to say they
helped carry them through
Now I see in his eyes speaking hurts too much
My heart is breaking

Kryptonite is pulverizing him, kicking him while he's down
He builds a force field of protection behind eyelids his pain can't find him in the dark
But I'm selfish, I flip the switch and take away his only weapon against kryptonite
Leading pain straight to him
I want him to know that I was here
I call out his name and yell SUPERMAN don't give up
Grasping his hand so tight trying to squeeze him back to normal, my normal, my healthy upbeat grandfather, my hero
His heart was his cape, and he wrapped me in it well protecting me from danger, he never let it fall
All I had to do was call, and he would swoop in to save the day
Like when I was 4 and I would see ghosts, my grandad would put on his cape and scare the ghost away
Or the time he saved me from metro, by driving from Louisiana to Houston to buy me a car for college and driving back the same day.

70

I grasp his hand even tighter, begging please wake
up
He squeezes back my heart smiles
Flashing back to the days when he would take me
to get Icee's, I lived for those days, my sister and I
riding on the back of his truck, my granddaddy
always had a truck
My superman would tell me that the world was
mine, everything was mine and he did his best to try
to give it all to me
They say he spoiled me, but they don't know the
connection between me and my superman
Just as quickly as he came, he left again
Fading into darkness with eyes wide open
I see my eyes looking into his looking at me
Yet my name escapes his memory
Just last week I was on the phone with him,
having a normal conversation
And last month he was joking with me saying I
must have used grease to get into my skinny jeans
Now I'm carrying a stranger's face
He's disconnecting from his reality, he is tired of
suffering

I see Superman letting go
My heart can't take the pain
Cancer, I mean kryptonite, I mean cancer doesn't
fight fair
Revealing his inner Clark Kent
Stripping him of his strength
He's losing the battle, his bodily functions are
fleeting
His organs gave up on him
GOD, I don't want to give up on him
I watched his cape fall
Now Superman can't save himself and as much as I
want to, I can't save Superman
My heart stopped beating
I watched Kryptonite Defeat Superman

ABANDONED MEMORIES

Abandoned memories cling to hope that one day
she'll realize they're missing
Bewildered, confused
She looks like my Grandmother, she sounds like my
Grandmother
But my Grandmother would never
She would never allow anyone to see her looking
like this
She would never do something like that
She would never…
Her thoughts travel aimlessly through time
Reliving that moment from 50 years back so vividly
Yet she can't retain the conversation we had five
minutes ago
Today she couldn't remember what she recalled so
easily last night
She is so much more coherent at night
At night she is the grandmother I remember
During the day I am the granddaughter she doesn't
But she always remembers her praying great-
granddaughter Kari

During the day, at night whenever she remembers
Kari
Sometimes when I call her, I have to say, Hey
Granny, it's me Chris, your first grandchild
Kari's Mom…. And she responds, Oh my praying
grandbaby. How are you doing?
My heart breaks when I see her this way
My Grandmother was a teacher until she retired
And after she retired, she still taught
Raised and educated half of Minden, Louisiana
A small town outside of Shreveport where I'm from
For as long as I can remember until Covid my
Grandmother kept kids
She was always teaching
Made sure we said, Yes Ma'am, No Ma'am, yeah,
nah, huh, and what were unacceptable in her home
Prim and proper as they come
Never a hair out of place, nails always done
Well she still keeps those nails done
Remnants of my Grandmother remain
But some of herself she's forgotten
She asks a question, we answer, two minutes later,
the question is on repeat

We answer again and the cycle continues
She wanders inside of the house. She wanders
outside of the house.
She wonders where my Grandfather is who passed
away in 2013
And then she remembers he passed away in 2013
She wonders who all the people are in her house
Then she remembers we're her grandchildren
Her mind wanders, Her body wanders
I wonder where the grandmother is I remember
Always taking me to the casino whenever I get into
town
I called her "The Gambling Queen" because she'd
always win
She called me a 'Scary Gambler" because I was
afraid to lose
Now, she's lost in a familiar space
Cognitively declining with each passing day
Simple tasks are not so simple for her anymore
Assistance is required
They say there are 7 stages
Stage 1 isn't noticeable
Stage 2 can be contributed to getting older

Stage 3 may be slight cause for concern
Stage 4 at this stage you wonder how you missed
the signs from the previous 3 stages
Stage 5, this is where we are right now, the center
stage
Stage 6, we're not ready for stage 6
Stage 7, if we weren't ready for 6, 7 is
incomprehensible
Stuck center stage. We have questions from the
audience
We the family we're the audience
Is this hereditary? How did we miss this? Why isn't
there a cure for this?
Can her abandoned memories be recovered if she
doesn't know they exist?
There was just one answer
Her memories weren't abandoned, they were stolen
Dementia is a thief

HOME

Home is where my car is
It's where I keep my green duffle bag with my best
clothes packed tightly
My shirts rolled up as small as the packages of
underwear you buy at Walmart
See, that way I can fit three pairs of pants and
maybe squeeze in a dress or two
My undergarments are folded neatly into the side
pockets
Sometimes I can even fit two pairs of shoes, not
including the ones on my feet
My hygiene products, deodorant toothpaste, comb,
brush, and soap.
I put those items in the other side pocket of my
duffle bag
The rest of my wardrobe I keep in my closet which
doubles as my trunk
I sit in my favorite chair, also known as the driver's
seat
I drive aimlessly up and down highways

Finally take an exit and find myself at the
intersection of pride and making the backseat my
bed
I'm hit by darkness which forces me to turn on the
lights
Bypass pride and turn to a friend for help
I arrive at a place to stay for a night or two
But I never get too comfortable, don't want to
overstay my welcome
After my stay is over, I return to my home parked
outside
I drive to my storage building to refill my clothes,
contemplate staying there.
But my nerves won't let me
So, I just sit outside of my storage building.
Listening to my home entertainment system
You call it a radio
Finally, I move my mobile home to the street
before the storage gates lock for the night
And I try to figure out where I will park tonight.
This is my routine because home is where my car is,
which makes me one of the lucky ones
At least I have a shield from the rain, heat and cold

I can lock my doors when I sleep for many others
Home is where the clothes on their back is
Or where the box, they found on the street is
Or where the police won't kick them out of is
Or where the person they are running from can't
find them is
I could never feel sorry for myself.
Because even though for a while home was where
my car was at least I had a home, friends, and family
to call on
I'll never forget when home was where my car was

NO ONE KNEW

No one knew
No one knew what she knew to be true
No one knew what she was going through
No one knew what she had already been through
No one knew how much pain she went through
No one knew that there was something they could
do
No one knew what she was keeping inside
No one knew that she was on an emotional
rollercoaster ride
No one knew that before she went to sleep each
night she cried
No one knew that she searched for somewhere to
hide
No one knew that she needed someone on her side
No one knew that she had been swallowing her
pride
No one knew that to keep her scars hidden she lied
No one knew that her sweet spirit had died
No one knew that her river of hurt ran so wide
No one knew that she wanted to leave, she tried
and tried

No one knew that she felt like she was in a place where she didn't belong
No one knew that she felt like something was wrong
No one knew that she felt this feeling so strong
No one knew that she felt like she didn't have very long
No one knew that she tried her best to hold on
No one knew that she was fighting this battle on her own
No one knew that she was all alone
No one knew the suffering she kept to herself
No one knew that she was crying out for help
No one knew that she thought her unspoken words were clear
No one knew that she was desperate for someone to hear
No one knew that she had been living in fear
No one knew that she felt like the end was near
No one knew that she had cried her last tear
No one knew until she was no longer here
No one knew

(This is dedicated in loving memory of my sister Rozetta, and to all the women and families who were, and are victims of domestic violence, please tell someone)

AS SHE LAY

As She Lay
Lay there with no more words to say
Lay there not of her own free will
Lay there motionless and still
As She Lay
Lay somehow always knowing that it would end up
this way
Lay there in this very strange place
Lay there with no emotion in her face
As She Lay
Lay there with the pain slowly going away
Lay there, no longer able to hide her scars
Lay there after putting up a good fight but not
winning the war
As She Lay
Lay there knowing that no matter how much she
wanted to she could no longer stay
Lay there knowing she would not get a chance to
say goodbye
Lay there with no more tears left to cry
As She Lay

Lay there on that Christmas day
Lay there knowing that this day would never again
be the same
Lay there praying that everyone would get through
all the hurt and pain
As She Lay
Lay there and for her loved ones she continued to
pray
Lay there praying that through this trying and
difficult time that they would be strong
Lay there praying that they know that none of them
did anything wrong
As She lay
Lay there waiting to be carried away
Lay there and her whole life flashed before her eyes
Lay their asking for forgiveness for telling and
believing other people's lies
As She Lay
Lay there with no prayers left to pray
Lay there now able to release
Lay there, after all the prayers, she finally received
her peace
As She Lay

ROSE

Rose by any other name wouldn't smell as sweet
Speaking of sweet
How fitting was it that you nick-named yourself
Sweet-P
You were proud to be short and petite
People didn't understand how such feistiness could
come from someone with such a small physique
And your presence could be felt as soon as you
walked into a room
With that contagious smile of yours you could turn
anyone's frown upside down
And your laughter, it could be heard from miles
away
You were always able to get people to listen to what
you had to say
And you loved with all your heart
The way you loved it was a form of art
And to be fortunate enough to experience your love
was a gift within itself
You were always the first one to offer someone in
need your help

Beautiful does not even begin to describe you
Your beauty wasn't restricted to the outside
Your beauty spread from the outside in
Your beauty was seen with every selfless act you
made
Your beauty was heard with each word of
encouragement you spoke
And the experiences that we shared, I wouldn't
have wanted to share them with anyone else
You would seldom complain when I was forced to
tag along
And as the years passed, you started inviting me on
your own
Encouraging me to tag along
But making me change clothes as soon as we left
home, I have to admit I was always scared that I'd
get caught
But with it I would go along, if it meant that I could
tag along
And that one time, we did almost get caught
But you somehow managed to figure a way out
You taught me more than any books could
I looked up to you just like a little sister should

And when I was younger, I tried to imitate your
ways, Even when I knew that it meant I would be
getting in trouble because I was following behind
you
And I call those the good old days
I would follow you always
I would've followed you to the end of the earth
And when you were taken from this earth
I didn't know how I could stay on it
You were my sister, My best friend, my lifeline
And all my memories on earth had you in them
So, I reached out to my lifeline, and I felt your spirit
say that I could go on
And that from now on
You would be the one that was tagging along

MATERNITY LEAVE

I wish America knew
Maternity isn't something I can leave
It's not a vacation I will return from
I may be back at work, but maternity hasn't left
It doesn't magically disappear when I clock in
Motherhood never clocks out
I wish America knew A mother's worth
12 weeks of unpaid leave is an insult
You get paid to go on vacation
Paid when you're sick
But when you bring life into the world, nothing
Securing my job shouldn't be my only
compensation
I really wish America knew
12 weeks' leave isn't long enough
For 40 weeks, that's 10 months if you go the full
term of your pregnancy
In my case 39 weeks and 5 days out of 48 weeks in
the year
I spent every week, every hour, every minute, every
second with this life

Growing inside of me from the size of a tadpole to an actual human being
Feeling each kick, each punch in my ribs,
Every new dance step she took on my bladder
I felt this every day for almost an entire year
And when she came out, I got to match her face to each kick, each punch, each dance step
I'm looking at my heart beating
I wish America knew
The first 3 months of motherhood are the hardest
Learning how to be responsible for someone other than yourself
Making sure you don't break them
You're not sleeping, she's not sleeping
Trying to remember to eat, remember to breathe
Learning how to nurture this tiny little person you brought into this world
Crying in the middle of the night because you can't remember which position worked better for nursing, which side you used the last time
Is she getting enough milk
Has it been 2 hours yet or has she transitioned to 3
Trying to pump while she sleeps

Why is she crying I just changed her, fed her
What I am supposed to do
All while your body is trying to recover from giving
birth
And once you finally start to get it a little together
In the middle of becoming maternal, leave
I really wish America knew
A woman should not be expected to return to work
when a part of her soul is missing
A body can't function without its heart
America, I wish you knew better

MOTHER MAY I

Mother May I
Mother may I take one step forward towards you to
say how eternally grateful I am to you for choosing
to give life to me, when the doctors told you it
would be better for your health if you killed me
Mother may I take two steps forward and say how
much I respect you
A single Mother of three girls, we may have wanted
some extras, but you always surpassed our needs
Mother may I take three steps forward to tell you
how much I appreciate all the sacrifices you made,
You gave up your dreams to help ours come true
Mother may I take four steps forward to thank you
for teaching me how to be a lady,
How to carry myself with respect, and how to love
myself
Mother, may I take five steps forward to say to you,
you are the strongest person I know, not many

people could have as much strength as you demonstrated after the tragic loss of your first-born child.

That was truly a remarkable sight to see

Mother may I take six steps forward to attempt to count the number of times you have helped me get out of situations that I thought would get the best of me

Mother may I take seven steps forward to thank you for all the prayers you prayed for me and continue to pray for me

And at the same time thank you for teaching me how to pray

Mother may I take eight steps forward to say, now I understand why you kept us in the church

I saw the faith you have in God, and I knew I wanted to be just like you some day

Mother may I take nine steps forward to say I'm grateful that I had you as an example of what it

means to pursue your dreams no matter what
anyone else has to say
Mother may I take ten steps forward to say you are
my inspiration, the reason why I write
I saw how passionate you were with your writing,
and you showed me I could do the same
Mother may I take eleven steps forward to say I
can't tell you how much your words of
encouragement truly encourages me
Sometimes you believe in me more than I believe in
myself
Mother may I take twelve steps forward to tell you
how blessed I am to have you as my mother
God created the best gift when he created you and
then he allowed me to come through you
Mother may I take thirteen steps forward to show
you how much I abundantly love you
I love you just for being you

Mother may I take fourteen steps forward to say
thank you for modeling exactly what a mother
should be
You taught me how to be a mother before I even
knew I even wanted to be
Kari reaps the benefits of the great Mother you
showed me how to be
And I continue to reap the benefits of the Amazing
Mother you are to me.

SENSES OF LOVE

Feels like excitement, fear, and anxiousness rolled
into one
Sounds like God was listening
Smells like a blessing brewing
Look like the word pregnant spelled out on a clear
blue stick
Tastes like miracle, As I digest God's will

Tases like happiness on my tongue, telling my
Husband I'm pregnant
Feels like a second chance
Sounds like Thank you God
Smells like a breath of fresh Grace
Looks like Joy

Looks like a rainbow, that's what they call a baby
conceived after miscarriage
Tastes like Hope
Feels like Faith
Sounds like No weapons formed against this baby
will prosper

Smells like promise

Smells like Favor
Tastes like obedience following God's plan
Looks like Mercy in an ultrasound
Feels like protection in my womb
Sounds like Heaven

Sounds like hearing her heartbeat for the first time
every time
Smells, smells like, smells like, smells like
everything, I literally smell everything
Looks like being a Superhero, my superpower is
growing a human inside of me
Tastes like craving pineapples and chocolate at 2
AM
Feels like breaking water

Feels like my heart is beating outside of my body
Sounds like freedom
Smells like peace
Looks like God's promise fulfilled
Tastes like happy tears

Tastes like the sweetest thing I've ever known
Feels like holding the answer to my prayers
Sounds like triumph
Smells like innocence
My Daughter looks like what love would look like if
love had a face

REFLECTION OF LOVE

Me - She's my heart beating outside of my body
Kari - mommy is the joy of my day.
Me - She's God's promise fulfilled
Kari - mommy is my number #1 wish.
Me - She's my dream come true
Kari - mommy is the power source of my heart.
Me - Kari is the light when darkness tries to surround me
Kari - mommy is my dream of my life that make love surround me.
Me - Kari is proof that love exists
Kari - mommy is and always be my joy and star.
Me - Kari is the gift that never stops giving,
Kari - my mom is the best mom that ever exist she is the best of the best.
Me - Kari is the answers to my prayers
Thank you Kari for choosing me to be your Mom

(Written by My Daughter and myself, intentionally left her words as she typed them at age 8)

ENDLESS THOUGHTS

My mind is a roaming soul painting new adventures
with my thoughts
Fervently taking me around the world that exists in
my head
Looking over the yellow caution tape warning me
of dangerous outcomes
Strokes of Stop Sign Red stands out on those
decisions that I know better than to make
But all I see are the specs of green telling me to go
My thoughts know no bounds
They color outside of the lines
Drawing conclusions along the way
They travel down their own path
Willing to take on whatever challenges come with
the journey to greatness
Navigating this route by following my own intuition
Creating purpose by letting my thoughts take the
wheel
Arrive at a canvas of abundance
My thoughts are endless

ABOUT THE AUTHOR

Chrishonda "Chris Crawford" Smith has been writing poetry and short stories since childhood. Chris has had poetry published in local magazines and newspapers. Chris Crawford has had the privilege of sharing her poetry in front of live audiences for several years. Chris has always had a passion for all things creative.

Chris Crawford is not only a writer and spoken word performer, but she is also a photographer. The photography of Chris Crawford has been displayed on numerous occasions in the Museum of Fine Arts Houston. Chris created the cover for this book and her very talented daughter Kari took the photograph of her mother for this book. This is the first of many books to come from Ms. Chris Crawford.